Birds of a Feather

Poems by

Lynn Martin

Birds of a Feather

ISBN 978-0-9852380-1-8

Cover art by Tarn Martin

To my children,
Ian, Tad, and Tarn

and my friend,
Anne Alexander

Table of Contents

Accidentals

Something out of place,
seen where it doesn't belong.

A surprise on the water
like Tundra Swans unexpected
and flung far from the Arctic
onto a Vermont pond.

Me, driving home, seeing all that white
with sinewy S-shaped necks
out of the corner of my eye.

Blessed is an ordinary Wednesday,
now etched forever in memory
as <u>that</u> Wednesday I went home

another way and found myself
far flung from work, from home,
from whoever I was before

black beaks beckoned me
while four pairs of wings unfolded.

Out of the Wilderness

You are perfect in your element:
honed sixty million years ago

zipped feathers, solid bones,
a black and white reflected shadow.

Unnoticed on a winter ocean
in a drab, gray and white coat,

the common loon, like the prince of story,
each spring transforms, floats forward into glory,

returns north to fresh water
builds a nest on almost land

inches away from a dive no predator can follow.
It's call tingles the spine,

tremolo of longing,
out of the wilderness, I'm here, where are you?

Male and female they share sitting on the nest.
Watery green flecked with dark spots,

the eggs lie in sedge and moss,
carefully concealed for twenty-nine days,

The adults, always vigilant for gulls, skunks, minks, weasels.
One day old the baby plops into water.
And that's the end of land.

Out of the wilderness, I'm here, where are you?
Sixty million years from now

who will answer?

A bird in the house

Was it a sliver of doubt you followed
squeezed sideways through a window
to flutter along the walls of my life?

Ours eyes meet.
You turn aside
recognizing something foreign.
Even the green shadow of afternoon
can't pale the blue gaze of fear.

You want to end the conversation.
It doesn't interest you, this almost
knowing clouds and wind direction.

Exhausted you fly behind shutters,
beat at the air with weakened wings,
trapped in a corner and panting,

where finally I hold you in my hand,
a piece of the world new to me,
heart beat so fast I fear for your life.

Have I ended any dialogue
we might have had between breaths?

Gently I place you outside
You lie still as death.

Then, in an upright flash of light
reversed, you dart into a sky
intended to mirror the smallness of me

left behind. My fingers stare speechless
already folded around the loss
of a handheld song, those few notes

your heart played against my questioning palm.

A song about a walk

Puffs of snow
  as if the trees were breathing
    fell delicately down.

Up there, nearly hidden,
  a flock of blue jays
    muttered their silent way,

over a quiet figure looking up.
  Someone out for a walk
    for the sheer love of it.

And the sight of bluewings in so much white
  tightened his heart to singing
    perhaps for the first time in days.

The birds paid no attention
  going their avian way
    full bellied and ready for sleep.

He was no danger to them
  so still in the twilight
    looking up as the snow came down.

The jays didn't associate him with
  chainsaws or the sudden absence
    of trees. For that matter

he didn't either. And yet that's all
  it would take for one more brightness
    to fade away.

Months later, maybe years
  he'd remember a day
    when something of such deep color

had passed overhead and healed him
  with a harsh talking to itself
    sending puffs of snow

earthward to settle on
  his shoulders with exquisite touch.
    And, then again, maybe he wouldn't.

As the crow flies

Out of a green cave, the crows call, marking the day,
giving it some kind of border, some form
                              in the struggle to begin.

        Last night, down by the river, thirty crows flew overhead,
    evening flocking like black clouds gathering,
a definite destination in their silent flight and fringed wings.

        Not like these early morning barkers, sitting
                    outside my window insisting, "Listen."
    Their ebony bodies glow with mystery,
        some secret they tell each other over and over.

        Not a warning, since the little birds
                ignore the frenzied commands. More like invitation:
        sound in the morning to declare place, silence in the evening
                    offering distance and departure.

This morning they own the tracery of leaves,
            poised on the edge of my ears almost understanding,
                            almost there.

Thousands of years ago, our genes would have heard
                and deciphered.

The day would have been planned between the cries
and the silence.
We would have moved in tune with the crows' hoarse advice.

We remember, somewhere, I know we do, how to live in the
same green world, the same blue sky, the same easy
transformation between life, death, grief and joy.

Can you tell me what they are saying?
I need to know what they are saying.

Science Lesson grades K-4, 7-9 pm
an evening with the Vermont Institute of Natural Science

The natural science man watches the faces
    row upon row of children there for the show.
       Presto, like a magician, his hand disappears into a box
          which only minutes ago shook with a ghostlike rattle
   and a shriek none of us recognized from hard backed chairs,
     school protected and yet Shazam
        produces its miracle
           no less
as on his arm sits a barn owl
     rescued from an unnatural grounding
       with a bullet hole in its wing.

None of this touched the eyes
     boring into ours across a space immense.
     Proud, of itself, dismissing schools,
              in one imperious blink.

  We all hold our breath, stunned into attention.

This bird carries the sun on its back, mottled
    like the beams and shadows of a tree canopy,
      evolved to fool any overhead hunter bigger than an owl.

We are looking at the ages,
    time beyond knowing, sitting on a man's arm
      and the children are seers emerging.

We stare at each other,
    the owl and us,
      transported out the doors, high above the earth
        watching ourselves on school chairs
            as seen in a bird's eye.

The children are quiet, looking up.
    The bird looks down.

Night of the owl

Dark on dark in a rainy gloom,
shadow swoops crisscrossed branches,
like a prisoner let loose
after the winds.

Down on a branch she raises a wing,
carelessly sifts feathers
with a beak hooked lethal,
watching me with indifferent eye.

Strange creature abroad
on a night touched by a fractured moon,
inscrutable her intent,
but comforting.

Living with animals

Maybe it's that old story of rescue
Lassie. Rin Tin Tin,
the two dogs and the Siamese cat
on a long walk back, looking for home

Or it could be a fixed point in the day,
sureness of warmth, need,
a timetable, yes
a timetable

It's not an easy world as we all know
You turn around and you are old,
or sick, or hurting; reaching out
to whatever reaches back

Feathers and fur talk of the now,
keep us humble in the minute,
because they must be fed,
walked, played with
in exchange for a love
that has no limits

Immune systems may be erratic,
the very planet may wobble,
yet this day begins with a squawk,
a bark, a wet tongue

I open my eyes; I am alive.

Repeating pattern

A robin
flings himself
at my back window,
his territory threatened
by his own image
staring back.

This is no small thing!
He returns
for three years
to the same place,
the same rival.

And what a rival !

Equal in intent,
unvanquished
they meet head on
over and over
until light changes
and the double vanishes.

Next day the same again,
until summer
thrusts him blindly
on his way to other things.

Little narcissus of the morning,
do you dream through the winter
of returning and finding yourself
king of the hill?

Certainly he survives
to return unchanged, unyielding

and with such pride!

Like a blue heron under a wide sky
for Damaris

Sometimes,

like when the blue heron
stands so still
the world stops,
and contracts to
a blue cascade of feathers,
so concentrated in intent,
everything holds its breath,

I meet someone
dressed in a blue skirt
and I hesitate
asking where
have I met her before,
where have I seen her
standing quiet and
centered on her feet,
familiar in the way her body
leans toward something
I can't see?

Just as the heron
will open its wings
and suddenly double its size,
so, also, does she
step forward, turn to an audience,
lean into song,
doubled with the weight of all of us,
who yearn to fly.

How vulnerable are the creatures of the sky,
visible against a blue so wide,
they have no choice,
but to be who they are,
mysterious and connected
to the unseen pull of whatever god
had the imagination to create
a woman at once so herself,
and so much more.

The Adirondacks

We have left New Hampshire behind us
among the shaken leaves, waiting at the border
to welcome us back. But for now we play pioneer
and search for the holy grail. All the elements are here:
water disappearing around corners blown fast
against oars; a boat whose nose sniffs
and retreats from waves arcing their backs
in the shimmering light; an overland hike
whose roots kiss our boots in toestopping rapture;
the upper lake to cross before we are there.

Above our heads the mountains sit, hands folded
in a contemplation so severe the silenced ear struggles
to comprehend a world so ancient and still.
Under those eyes we wrestle to keep
our direction true, try not to get lost
in the deliberate beat of a blue heron's flight.
Somewhere an owl hoots the time. Nothing has begun,
nothing ended. We dip our paddles into the past,
chant an ancient litany:
Haystack, Basin, Saddleback,
Gothics, Sawtooth;
rediscover prayer.

Chickadees chatter a story of smallness
we can retell any way we please.
Everything listens and gives it back again.
Ravens drag the day reluctantly from one shore to the other.
Tonight it will snow. Tomorrow it will melt
every track, erased before we even open our eyes.

Rivers never say good-bye

Because it is afternoon,
the reeds part,
reveal a scene
from ancient Egypt
transposed onto the hot back
of a Vermont river.

A profile
with beak,
one eye
regal in its stillness,
steel-gray wings
folded like a morning coat,
stilt legs thrust into water
in an exact copy
of the cattail's grasp:

a blue heron.

We gasp
at this invitation
into the mysterious,
the hidden surprise,
provided by an eye centered promise
of exultation.

This is what it means
to be friends,
to stand fast
in the passing
of possible danger.

You are leaving
for another country.
I will remain.
The choice is ours:
to fold back into ourselves

or give a shout
and explode the heron
into the air
visible to all.

The bird
will rise, rise, rise
with long, even beats of its wings,
to disappear into our memories.

Wherever you go,
remember, my friend,
some things are eternal.

On the coldest day I need

Why do some birds disappear
arrowing the Connecticut
abark in the night sky
with our hearts so filled with longing ?

Did they have a long ago convention and decide
this one goes south; this one to the opposite pole,
this one to Jersey?

I find it hard to let go of those who leave,
especially the robin who has been my friend for months.
I brood and plot revenge on those who fade into darkness,
those many-hued beauties whose songs
float me out the door on summer days.

I know your kind I rant:
Yellow-rumped and tanager.
As soon as the going gets rough,
you are gone.

I celebrate stick-to-it-ness.
Blue jay, who totes the sky to ground,
Downy and hairy and pileated woodpecker,

Tufted titmouse who is always here, here, here.
The white and red-breasted nuthatches,
Sparrows and chickadees,

the ones you can count on
because
it's on the coldest day I need.

2 crows 2 squirrels

Cold
        ice covered earth
                        backyard drifts
Power outrages
        trees down
                        cold cold winter

Huddled at the window
I watch 2 crows and 2 squirrels
forage the snow drifts
for anything the snow hasn't swallowed:
old seeds, bread crumbs, half eaten nuts.

It's just another day in December.

Crow is black, shiny with light.
Squirrel's tail is a burst of white.

Cardinal Delight

Astride the green leaves,
the fire-bird's clear notes

create light.
My ear turns to the blaze,
songed into hearing.

With heart stopping whistle,
he burns with Now. Right now
Do it now.

I am standing in Austin Dickinson's house,
listening to stories of the sister next-door.

When I look up,
I am stunned by red
looking back at me through window glass.

Perched on a blowing branch,
it has to be her.

Feathered in cardinal delight,
I hold my hands toward
possibility,

that bird
amid the solitary green,
alone within the centuries.

Visiting Edna St. Vincent Millay

The snow had its surface whipped and frozen last night.
Bad weather for deer, who no matter how delicate
their feet, break through and cannot
out run anything. A short dash ends beneath pines
where like shadows that breath, they wait.
The little food left has been locked in by a wind
who didn't care enough to stay and watch.
A beech tree shivers in a brown imitation
of a summer nothing can imagine.
Snowshoes are dangerous these days,
the tips catching at each step.
It's imperative to move with great care

down the path winding past birches
whose ragged bark hangs loose
like my skin under all these clothes
waiting for a sun warm enough to resurrect belief
in something more than hunched shoulders
and gray dawns. Where is this path leading?
I decide it doesn't matter, just as I come
into a clearing empty of trees, with only
the yellow straw of summer's last grass
bent over in conversation with a weary chain,

marking the circumference of a burial plot,
mounded and laid with a blanket of white
as if winter provided warmth right here
and in so doing wiped out the name
of whoever sleeps here, or is this winter's ,
sense of humor, carelessly creating its own symbol,
but winter always overdoes it, must hammer home
a message we prefer to forget. Tight to a branch,
a tiny bird holds fast with frozen claws,
thin beak open in amazement at the sky.
So many ways to sing!

Slow as I am moving,
I can give this grave a name and talk
of tomorrow. Winter's hold is already broken.
Snow gives grudgingly beneath my feet.
From a hidden corner a chickadee calls.
Everything bends to listen.

A certain Mark Doty sky

Birds eat their own weight in food every day, which seems
easy for the chickadee, impossible
for the jay, yet it's the same,

an endless search for nourishment, an ache,
Mark's voice an overlay of dream like a soft whirr
of wings overhead. Birds eat and eat and eat

their fill, grow silently restless after dark, till morning
eyes the leaf, yesterday obscure, suddenly individual,
like suddenly falling in love with someone not new to your life.

How do you do that? Resurrect the ordinary joy of one leaf?
You live among the highest branches of the tallest oak,
transform distance into light others don't understand, but feel.

It's too bad you can't hear your own poems being read by you,
the way they reverberate in the heart, until we are found
wandering against the sky, looking down at ourselves,

not unlike a flock of swallows eating out of your hand,
startled as if the song is ourselves,
and we are no longer afraid of the dark.

You create the whole bird from a flash of vermillion and azure fire.

Even a dead bird by the side of the road,
a tangle of mud and yellow feathers,
the beak twisted at an impossible angle,
comes alive under your spell. Listen Mark,
How simple:

"You thaw the air and it sings".

quote from *January, Waking,* by Mark Doty

Crow

carries on her back
all we don't know.
Heavy winged
she cleaves the sky
into rough edged nuggets
even our blind palms can read.
Have you noticed
she feeds by the side of the roads
in between arriving and departure,
her tongue harsh
as if the message she carries
has traveled from one soul to another?
Despite the infinite winds
of separation
she is our third eye
of connection.
She insists
on calling
until we look up
and listen.

Down the road from the elementary school

In the midst of mountains,
a quail at her feet,
jays shooed from feeders,
in a yard across from hayfields
newly shorn, down
the street from the elementary school,
grandkids tucked into desks,
all dreaming of riding the tractor
at four o'clock;
a woman waves.

It was the 60's in Vermont,
when all these strangers came to town.
Just moved in
leaving cities, traffic, jobs behind.
Came to help:
gather eggs
bring in the cows
carry milk
weed the garden
wash the veggies
stack them in the roadside stand.

The woman
dazzled by all our unknown voices
opened her arms and took us in,
women, men and children.
Fed us:
pickles
tomatoes
cauliflower
broccoli
lettuce
apple cider
maple syrup.

She patched everyone's jeans.
A Grameo patch we called it,
recognized all over town.
We were her kids
no matter our age,
held fast to the land
by a stitch in time.

Like an egg

I crack my car open
shatter glazed windows, smash
a mounded roof, set loose a buried hood
rediscover and unblind headlights,
all the while caught between
fragility and imminent destruction,
as if I needed to be reminded
how thintheline,

the same as when I take pen to paper,
stubborn, no matter what goes down,
what computer winks out.
Gloved or huddled by candlelight
makes no difference, my soul
insists on release.

Emily, I can understand why
you sewedthosebooks together,
wrote the desired against
the freezing night. If that's insanity
I choose it over pretense, voices insisting
there's nothing new under the sun.

If I have to crack cars open
to get where I'm going,
wear crampons to grip the ground,
don a hard hat
        as

             trees

                come

                    down
it's no different from trying to shape
this poem, walk it firm
to meet the dawn of any new beginning.

Among tornadoes, volcanoes, avalanches, nor'easters,
a hanging on, going on
with love a thin insulation
against the skin.

Grandfather Robin

Mygod,
at 4 a.m.
the robin's at it
off-key and with such passion.

He's the first up
and the last to bed
a regular, factory worker type bird
like my relatives

rising before daybreak
to make sneakers
or fill bottles of beer
or working

the late shift
racking up those pensions.
Health care junkies,
with two cars & a mortgage,

they all quit school at 16,
put their pay in my grandmother's hand,
till they married and moved out,
one less mouth to feed

in a family of 17. All my uncles had
pride like the robin
orange breast aglow
in an off to work light

The girls were quiet. Good girls,
threading the bobbins
folding the boxes
packing auto parts

for shipment to the rest of the world
somewhere out there
beyond the factory,
like a picture on a calendar

hanging on a door,
advertising sneakers, beer
 auto parts, gorgeous
women in gilded dresses.

The early bird gets the worm,
my grandfather would say,
a regular robin type factory worker,
singing the American dream.

So how does that explain me
one generation away
a lesbian, who wears sneakers, drinks beer,
and buys a glitzy dress now & then?

I sleep through the robin's wake up call
every chance I get.
The America my family built
wishes I'd go away.

My relations won't say the L word,
vote Republican with pride,
but they're stuck with me
because of grandpa,

who, like the robin, fed his young
each and every one,
even the occasional cowbird
mistaken in the nest.

We belong.
Even Bobby who OD'ed on heroin,
Even Sara who is Portuguese,
even me.

So what if we sing
a little off key
Grandpa says,
Family is Family.

Make a joyful noise

It's hanging onto a reed, so, at first, I think it must be
a red-wing blackbird. There are red-wings everywhere, landing
and bending reeds in their travels to and fro over this backwater
swamp. This bird is about the same size, but it is not black.
Its bright orange legs grasp the reed like an over-sized grasshopper.
Fierce eyes glint like metallic rays, and its chest gleams as if
molten in the sun. As I watch, a needle thin bill lifts to the sky.
AWK, it croaks. That's it.

I am looking at a green heron. I've seen them lurking
on the edges of the swamp, but never in the open like this.
Now I begin to feel uncomfortable, like an intruder, like a binocular
voyeur intruding on some kind of praise song. And I am suddenly
bereft, missing something, and AWKless in my human skin.

www.ingramcontent.com/pod-product-compliance
Lightning Source LLC
Chambersburg PA
CBHW031634040426
42452CB00007B/828